The New-Wave
MAI TAI

The New-Wave MAI TAI

CHERYL CHEE TSUTSUMI

WATERMARK
PUBLISHING

Hats off to the imaginative mixologists who ventured outside
the box to create the new-wave mai tais in this book.
Mahalo also to Hukilau restaurant in downtown Honolulu for
providing the setting; ingredients; glassware; and bartenders
Thomas Blasque, Joe Toro and Emerson Lewis for our
three-day photo shoot.

- Cheryl Chee Tsutsumi

Compilation © 2008 Watermark Publishing

Text © 2008 Cheryl Chee Tsutsumi

Design
Leo Gonzalez

Production
Marisa Oshiro

Drink photography
David Croxford

ISBN 978-0-9815086-1-0

Library of Congress Control Number:
2008927497

Printed in Korea

Watermark Publishing
1088 Bishop Street, Suite 310
Honolulu, Hawai'i 96813
Telephone 1-808-587-7766
Toll-free 1-866-900-BOOK
sales@bookshawaii.net
www.bookshawaii.net

Contents

Introduction

Okay, I admit it. I was born and raised in the Islands, but I never sipped a mai tai—a Hawaiian icon—until I started doing research for this book.

The reason? I've always regarded it as a humdrum "tourist drink" without the sauciness of a margarita, the sprightliness of a mimosa or the sophistication of a martini.

Nothing could be farther from the truth. The mai tai can be all of those things—and much more. In fact, it's a bit of an enigma. In an August 16, 2003 essay titled "Mixology Research: The Mai Tai" (www.drinkboy.com), Robert Hess observed, "The mai tai is a classic cocktail whose original recipe has unfortunately been randomized through a clumsy hand-me-down process, until such a point that many bartenders don't know (or often don't even care) as to how it is properly made."

Because of this, the mai tai hasn't always received the respect it deserves. Film critic, writer and actor Joe Bob Briggs dismissed the mai tai as "a combination of cough syrup, pancake batter and the automatic transmission fluid from a 1973 Oldsmobile Toronado."

In his book *Drinkology: The Art and Science of the Cocktail*, author James Waller called the mai tai "about as Polynesian as a plastic lei, inflatable palm trees or Hawaiian Punch (whose taste it inadvertently mimics). It's the kind of drink—decorated with paper parasols and other kitschy paraphernalia—that loud, loudly dressed, tourist-types used to guzzle too many of. The mai tai is, in a word, awful."

Mai tai aficionados, however, stand by their drink and have clear ideas about what constitutes a memorable one. It starts with premium rum and fresh ingredients (that means freshly squeezed juices and no syrups); it attains a nice balance of sweet and sour (a common error is to make the drink too sweet); and it is served cold (the ice can be shaved, crushed or in cubes, as long as there is a generous amount of it).

Other than that, when it comes to making mai tais, there apparently are no boundaries, no hard-and-fast rules, allowing creative mixologists to reinvent the world's most famous cocktail over and over again.

While purists stick to the traditional ingredients (rum, orange curacao, orgeat, simple syrup and lime juice), others have boldly experimented with flavorings as diverse as blueberry preserves, sherbet, li hing mui powder, ginger and Jell-O. Have fun mixing and tasting the 53 "new-wave" mai tai recipes I've selected for this book.

Cheers!
Cheryl Chee Tsutsumi

History of Rum

Rum is the mai tai's key ingredient—without question its heart and soul. Any mixologist will tell you a good rum is the basis of a great mai tai.

A colorful cast of characters, from sailors and slavers to buccaneers and bartenders, wrote rum's incredible history, which includes enough intrigue, excitement and drama to fill the screenplay for a Hollywood blockbuster.

Most rum is made from molasses, the thick brown syrup that remains after crystallized sugar is extracted from boiled cane juice. More than 50 percent of molasses is sugar, but it also contains significant amounts of calcium, magnesium, potassium, iron, and other minerals and trace elements that can contribute to rum's flavor. It takes about 1½ gallons of molasses to make a gallon of rum at 50 percent ABV (alcohol by volume).

The "wash" (mix of molasses and water) is fermented for a set period; depending on the type of rum being made, it ranges from 24 hours for subtle, light varieties to several weeks for rich, full-bodied ones. The rum is then distilled. Interestingly, all rums emerge from the still as clear, colorless liquids. Aging in wooden casks (sometimes for as long as 20 years) and the addition of caramel determine the final taste, color and body of the brew.

Thus, it's impossible to delineate a description for rum, for its styles are as varied as the people who make them.

Likewise, historians have been unable to determine exactly when and where rum was born. Fermented drinks made from sugarcane juice— the forerunners of rum—were enjoyed in India, China and Southeast Asia thousands of years ago. Although Portuguese colonists in Brazil or settlers in Spanish-held Hispaniola or Cuba may have invented rum as we know it sometime in the 17th century, it's widely accepted that rum was first mentioned in writing in the British colony of Barbados. An anonymous resident observed in 1651: "… the chief fuddling they make in the island is rumbullion, alias kill-devil, and this is made of sugar canes distilled, a hot, hellish and terrible liquor."

Rumbullion, a British slang word meaning "a great tumult or uproar," was shortened to "rum" by 1658. That was the year a deed for the sale of the Three Houses Plantation on Barbados mentions "four large … cisterns for liquor for rum." This is the first known official use of the word.

True to its forbidding nickname, "kill-devil," rum was at the outset very strong and unpleasant in taste. A severe hangover was the probable outcome for anyone who indulged in too much of it. On the bright side,

Mount Gay has been making rum in Barbados for more than 300 years.

because it was so potent, rum numbed both physical and emotional pain, making it useful as a medicine.

Rum-making techniques were refined over the years, yielding more palatable results. Mount Gay in Barbados claims to be the oldest rum maker in the world; it celebrated its 300th anniversary in 2003. Although Barbados and its Caribbean neighbors remain the undisputed hub of rum production, countries all over the globe are now making notable products, including Australia; Bermuda; Guyana; Guatemala; Nicaragua; Brazil; Venezuela; Tahiti; Thailand; the Philippines; and Florida, New Orleans and Hawai'i (see "Hawai'i's Rum Connections" on page 19) in the United States.

Following are other facts about rum that may surprise you.

Currency of the Slave Trade

By the 16th century, European powers were sending ships far beyond their home ports to lay stakes in exotic lands that held the promise of great riches. England, France, Spain and Portugal established a strong presence in the Caribbean islands, where a warm climate and abundant water sources provided the ideal conditions for growing cane. Plantations flourished there.

Sugar's success as a commodity encouraged planters to go one step further. They reasoned they could generate even more money if they expanded their focus to include rum, especially since it was made from a by-product of the sugar-manufacturing process that otherwise would be discarded. It took a while, however, for rum to gain a following. In 1698, England imported just 207 gallons of it, but less than a century later, demand had increased to more than two million gallons per year.

A huge workforce was needed to support the boom in sugar and rum production. In the 18th century, more than 4 million African slaves were

Workers tend to cane fields in Grenada, one of the top producers of rum in the world.

brought in as field workers for sugar colonies, primarily in British and French territories. How were they purchased? With Caribbean rum, at prices ranging from 200 to 225 gallons per slave in 1773.

The Grog Ration

During the 18th century, rum was a staple aboard British ships because it was relatively cheap and kept well. In contrast, fresh water would become musty and ridden with algae, especially in the warm, humid tropics. Although beer's alcohol content kept it from spoiling, its taste tended to decline on long voyages. And although sailors loved French brandy and Spanish wines, those libations were expensive and difficult to stock consistently.

By 1731, it was customary for British seamen to receive a half pint of rum every day at noon while at sea. The drink break lifted morale, eased tensions and promoted camaraderie between shipmates, and provided a brief

Grog rations aboard British Royal Navy ships were carefully portioned using metal cups such as this one.

British Admiral Edward Vernon was nicknamed "Old Grogram," from which the word "grog" was coined.

escape from the tedious routine of their lives. On the downside, lingering hangovers were common; tipsy sailors were more likely to be hurt while performing their duties; and, emboldened by the drink, a good number of them would go AWOL when their vessel dropped anchor at a port.

In addition, when his crews quaffed their ration at full strength, all at once, Admiral Edward Vernon (after whom Mount Vernon, George Washington's Virginia estate, was named) noticed "many fatal effects to their morals as well as their health, which are visibly impaired thereby." Rum, he added, caused a "stupefying [of] their rational qualities, which makes them heedlessly slaves to every passion."

To remedy the situation, Vernon issued an order at Port Royal, Jamaica on August 21, 1740, requiring the rum ration to be diluted with a quart of water. Sugar and lime juice, he said, could be added to make the drink taste better and to prevent scurvy. To further reduce the effects of the alcohol, the quota was to be split into two portions—one served between 10 a.m. and noon and the other between 4 p.m. and 6 p.m.

A dilemma arose: What should the new drink be called since it was no longer really rum? An unidentified sailor came up with the perfect answer. Because Vernon liked to wear a heavy waterproof coat made of grogram, a coarse wool and silk fabric stiffened with gum, he was known as "Old Grogram." "Grog" was coined from that moniker.

Vernon's grog order went into effect throughout the fleet and remained part of the Admiralty's naval code, albeit in reduced amounts, over the next 230 years. But as technical systems in the Royal Navy became more sophisticated, demanding mental acuity and keen judgment at all times, it no longer was wise to give grog to sailors on duty. Black Tot Day, July 31, 1970, was the last day sailors received grog rations. To mark the event, they wore black armbands and assembled for mock funerals on British ships around the world.

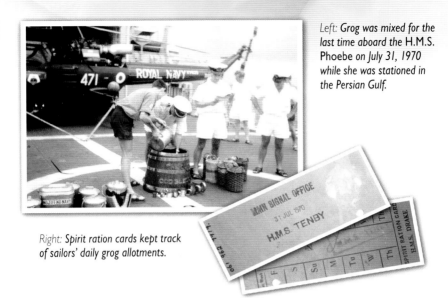

Left: *Grog was mixed for the last time aboard the* H.M.S. Phoebe *on July 31, 1970 while she was stationed in the Persian Gulf.*

Right: *Spirit ration cards kept track of sailors' daily grog allotments.*

The *H.M.S. Fife*, a guided missile destroyer, was berthed at Pearl Harbor—the closest vessel to the International Date Line and, accordingly, the last in the Royal Navy to dole out grog rations. In one of the most dramatic ceremonies of the day, her crew gathered on the top deck and tossed their rations, glasses and the whole rum barrel overboard to the sounds of a 21-gun salute.

Etymology of Eggnog

Come Christmas, Americans across the country raise glasses filled with eggnog. The rich, sweet drink laced with liquor has become as much a holiday tradition as caroling, mistletoe and gift exchanges.

Eggnog likely came to America from Europe with the colonists during the 17th century, since it mirrors many of the milk and wine punches that were popular among the aristocracy in the Old Country. Back then, only people of means could afford costly ingredients such as milk, cream, eggs, cinnamon, nutmeg, sugar, wine, brandy, whiskey and cognac.

But in the American colonies, many people farmed, providing a ready supply of eggs and dairy products. They used inexpensive rum in their eggnog instead of the other spirits, which were heavily taxed.

Some assert the drink was first named egg and grog, and as time went on, the words were combined to egg'n'grog, then eggnog. Others maintain "nog" comes from "noggin," a small wooden mug in which drinks were served at taverns. It's easy to see how an egg drink in a noggin would be called eggnog. The actual story might be a combination of those two explanations. Initially, the drink might have been dubbed "egg and grog in a noggin"—a mouthful that was sensibly shortened to eggnog.

Miracle after the Mutiny

On April 28, 1789, following the famous mutiny on the *H.M.S. Bounty*, Captain William Bligh and 18 crewmen loyal to him were set adrift in a 23-foot skiff. First Mate Fletcher Christian, leader of the mutineers, supplied them with twine, canvas, lines, sails, a tool chest, a compass, 150 pounds of bread, a 20-gallon cask of water and three gallons of rum.

After mutineers took command of H.M.S. Bounty *(pictured here), Captain William Bligh and those loyal to him were set adrift in a skiff with limited supplies, including three gallons of rum.*

Navigating by the sun, stars, currents and winds, Bligh and his men made an epic 46-day crossing over 3,600 miles of open ocean to safety in Timor, an island south of Indonesia. Every day during the voyage, the captain distributed a teaspoon of rum with a few sips of water and morsels of bread to each man. Amazingly, not a single sailor died during the ordeal, which Bligh attributed to this daily ration.

Rum and the Revolution

By 1690, rum was being manufactured in New England in ever-growing quantities, the centers for which were Newport on Rhode Island and Boston and Medford in Massachusetts. When the American Revolution erupted, there were 63 rum distilleries in Boston alone, and most colonists over the age of 15 were drinking nearly four gallons of it every year.

American life revolved around rum. A flagon of rum was on every table at mealtime. Sugar barons socialized and sealed deals over rum punches and toddies. Field workers woke up with a glass of rum and drank more of it during their breaks. Ministers boosted themselves with rum before giving their sermons, and it was served at every observance, from weddings to wakes.

In 1733, at the behest of British sugar plantation owners in the West Indies, England's parliament passed the Molasses Act, which imposed high taxes on molasses imported from non-British colonies. Since that molasses was cheaper (particularly from the Caribbean islands under French rule), the law was not embraced by the American colonies. It would have shut down New England's rum industry had smuggling and bribery of customs officials not kept producers stocked with cheap molasses.

Scholars believe rum played a major role in rousing the spirit of discontent that led to the American Revolution. John Adams, the charismatic leader of the movement who became the second president of the United States, stated, "I know not why we should blush to confess that molasses was an essential ingredient in American independence."

Patriotism was ignited in taverns, the nuclei of every town in the 13 colonies. Historian Charles Rorabaugh wrote: "… they were certainly seed beds of the Revolution, the places where British tyranny was condemned, militiamen organized and independence plotted. Patriots viewed public houses as the nurseries of freedom ..."

Samuel Adams and John Hancock organized the December 16, 1773 Boston Tea Party over drinks—including rum, no doubt—at Boston's Green Dragon Tavern. The Catamount Tavern in Bennington, Vermont was where Ethan Allen planned the successful May 10, 1775 raid on the British garrison of Fort Ticonderoga. While drafting the *Declaration of Independence* between June 11 and June 28, 1776, Thomas Jefferson frequented the Indian Queen Tavern in Philadelphia.

Rum also figured in stories about other famous Americans. Benjamin Franklin often used rum to negotiate treaties with the Indians. A chilling comment in his *Autobiography of Benjamin Franklin*, published in 1793, reads "indeed if it be the design of Providence to extirpate these savages in order to make room for cultivators of the earth, it seems not improbable that rum may be the appointed means."

In 1758, George Washington wooed voters with liquor to win a seat in Virginia's House of Burgesses, the first elected legislative assembly in the American colonies. The refreshments dispensed at the polls included 70

Above: In the 1770s, notable rum lovers such as Samuel Adams and John Hancock frequented the Green Dragon Tavern in Boston.

Inset: Thomas Jefferson was a regular at the Indian Queen Tavern in Philadelphia while he was drafting the Declaration of Independence *in June 1776.*

gallons of rum punch—a blend of rum, simple syrup, lemon and orange juices, nutmeg, cinnamon and cloves. The Father of Our Country was known to regularly buy large quantities of rum; for example, records show that in 1787, he purchased 491 gallons to distribute to his workers, both enslaved and free.

Before Paul Revere embarked on his midnight ride on April 18, 1775, he stopped at the home of Isaac Hall, captain of the Medford minutemen and owner of a rum distillery, where he fortified himself with a liberal serving of the spirit.

Yo-Ho-Ho, and a ...

Contrary to popular belief, rum wasn't linked to pirates until the 18th century. Rum wasn't part of the loot taken by the infamous 17th-century buccaneer Henry Morgan because it was not being produced on a large scale in the Spanish outposts in the Caribbean that he raided. While the Spanish did have sugar plantations there, rum production hadn't grown as it had in the British colonies because Spanish winemakers and brandy distillers, predicting serious competition from less expensive rum, were doing their best to prevent it.

Consequently, pirates found a lot of wine and brandy in the villages they plundered, but no rum. It was only when their attention turned to British holdings that they discovered rum, which from then on became closely associated with them and their high jinks on the high seas.

British buccaneer Edward Teach (1680-1718), immortalized as Blackbeard, earned notoriety not only for his barbarous deeds, but for his great fondness for rum. One of his favorite concoctions was gunpowder mixed with rum; he would ignite the cocktail and drink it while it burned and popped.

One of Blackbeard's favorite cocktails was made with rum and gunpowder.

The phrase "Yo-ho-ho, and a bottle of rum" can be traced to late summer 1881, when 31-year-old Robert Louis Stevenson was vacationing with his family at a cottage in Braemar in the Scottish Highlands. Although the young writer's career had not yet taken off, he knew the makings of a good story when he came across it. One cold, rainy afternoon, Stevenson saw his 12-year-old stepson, Lloyd Osbourne, painting a map of an imaginary island with watercolors. A plot began to form in Stevenson's mind as he studied the sketch, and he scribbled "Treasure Island" at the top right-hand corner of the paper. Within three days, with Lloyd's input, he had written the first three chapters of what was to become a literary classic.

Two weeks later, Stevenson's friend, Dr. Alexander Japp, took the initial chapters to *Young Folks* magazine. Intrigued, the editor agreed to publish the story, and, encouraged by that commitment, Stevenson finished it within two months. *Treasure Island* appeared as a weekly serial from October 1881 to January 1882, but, interestingly, it didn't receive much notice until it was republished in book form in 1883. It was Stevenson's first successful novel, and the words of the pirate Billy Bones became ingrained in every reader's head:

"Fifteen men on the dead man's chest
Yo-ho-ho, and a bottle of rum!
Drink and the Devil had done for the rest
Yo-ho-ho, and a bottle of rum!"

Composed by Stevenson, the ditty doesn't make much sense, although historians think it was based on an old sea chantey.

A Hero's Last Request

Admiral Horatio Nelson, one of Britain's greatest naval leaders, reputedly directed that if he were to die in battle, he wanted his body sent home in a barrel of rum. He didn't say this just for dramatic impact; in the early 19th century, rum was a cheap preservative and probably the only practical alternative to embalmer's fluid.

Led by Lord Nelson, the British navy won a decisive victory over French and Spanish forces at the Battle of Trafalgar on October 21, 1805, but at a great price: Nelson was shot dead by a sharpshooter late in the skirmish as his ship, *H.M.S. Victory,* passed the French vessel *Redoubtable.* Some accounts confirm that, in accordance with his wishes, his men did indeed place his body in a cask of rum for transport back to England.

During the voyage home, however, the sailors drilled a small hole at the base of the cask through which they drained most of the rum and drank it. They meant no disrespect to their fallen commander; rather, they thought they were being practical. Why let perfectly good rum just sit in the barrel? Since then, many old salts, especially those affiliated with the Royal Navy, often refer to rum as "Nelson's Blood."

The body of British Admiral Horatio Nelson, who was killed in the Battle of Trafalgar in 1805, supposedly was transported back to England in a cask of rum.

Rise of Rumrunners

Prohibition (January 16, 1920 to December 5, 1933) made it illegal for anyone in America to "manufacture, sell, barter, transport, import, export, deliver, furnish or possess any intoxicating liquor [defined as containing more than 0.5 percent alcohol]," with a few exceptions such as spirits used for religious rites and medicinal purposes.

That, however, didn't suppress the people's thirst for booze or their efforts to obtain it. Rumrunners—people and ships that carried prohibited liquor ashore or across a border—went into action. One famous Prohibition-era rumrunner was mobster Al Capone, who smuggled Cuban rum to Chicago from Mississippi beaches via Memphis and St. Louis. Although it was never proven, Joseph Patrick "Joe" Kennedy, Sr., patriarch of the prominent Kennedy clan, also reputedly made a fortune illegally importing alcoholic beverages from Canada during that period.

William Frederick "Bill" McCoy was an American boat builder and sea captain who ran rum-running operations between Florida and Bimini,

During the Prohibition era, rumrunners, including mobster Al Capone, made fortunes smuggling alcohol into the United States.

Left: This smuggler is wearing a multi-pocketed garment that could easily fit under a trench coat.

Above: Windsor, Ontario inspectors wait at a dock beside the Detroit River in 1928, hoping to stop mobsters' rum-running operations.

which, located 50 miles east of Fort Lauderdale, is the closest point between the Bahamas and the Mainland United States. McCoy was known as a fair dealer who only sold quality brands and never watered down his wares. Customers dubbed his shipments the "real McCoy," which is supposedly how that idiom came into common usage.

Presidential Favorite

In a June 30, 2007 *Wall Street Journal* article titled "As Polynesian as Nixon," writer Eric Felten reveals the mai tai was Richard Nixon's favorite drink. The president took his wife to Trader Vic's in Washington, D.C., on Valentine's Day in 1973, a week after the U.S. Senate, by a 77-to-0 vote, approved a resolution to form a committee to investigate Watergate.

The restaurant was a few blocks from the White House, in the basement of what was then the Statler-Hilton Hotel. "Nixon took the opportunity to enjoy a mai tai or two, and, in a clumsy effort at bonhomie, he backslapped his way out of the restaurant," reported Felten. "Stopping at a crowded table where a fresh round of mai tais had just been served, Nixon laughingly delivered a warning: 'They're lethal!'"

Felten goes on to note, "The mai tai became something of the official drink of the Nixon presidency, much to the consternation of some. When Pat Nixon would visit Trader Vic's with her husband, she stuck to Jack Daniel's. Nor was Daniel Patrick Moynihan a fan. U.S. ambassador to the United Nations, Moynihan would often fly down to Washington to meet with the president and Henry Kissinger after a week jousting with the perfidious Turtle Bay crowd.

"One such evening—after being stuck on the LaGuardia tarmac for hours—Moynihan found himself in an endless Kissinger confab. After a while, Moynihan realized he could use a drink. 'I told Henry I'd love a brandy,' the ambassador recalled to a writer for the *New York Times Magazine*. 'He sent his girl out to look for something.' It seems she went looking at Trader Vic's. 'She came back in about 20 minutes with some mai tai—that awful Chinese drink—which I had' (and you can just imagine the look on his face as he said it) 'in a plastic mug.'"

Make Hers a Mai Tai

Patty Hearst, the granddaughter of publishing magnate William Randolph Hearst, made front-page headlines for months during the mid-1970s. On February 4, 1974, members of the radical Symbionese Liberation Army (SLA) kidnapped the 19-year-old heiress from her Berkeley apartment. In early April, Hearst declared on an audiotape that she had joined the SLA and was now going by the name "Tania."

On April 15, surveillance cameras photographed Hearst wielding an assault rifle during a robbery of the Hibernia Bank in the Sunset district of San Francisco. In later taped communications, she reconfirmed her loyalty to the SLA, and a warrant was issued for her arrest.

Federal authorities captured Hearst and other SLA members in a San Francisco apartment in September 1975. The first thing she requested when she was released on bail was a mai tai.

Hearst was convicted of bank robbery on March 26, 1976 and sentenced to seven years in prison. On February 1, 1979, President Jimmy Carter commuted her sentence to time served, and she won freedom after spending just 22 months behind bars. On January 20, 2001, his last day in office, President Bill Clinton granted her a full pardon.

Heiress Patty Hearst was arrested in September 1975 for her role in a bank robbery five months earlier. The first thing she requested after posting bail was a mai tai.

Hawai'i's Rum Connections

Haleakalā Distillers

P.O. Box 1001, Kula, Hawai'i 96790
(808) 280-6822
www.mauirum.biz

Founded in 2003, Haleakalā Distillers produces five premium craft rums, all made with molasses from Hawaiian Commercial & Sugar Company's Pu'unēnē sugar mill. Its 155-proof DaBomb Extreme Rum, the strongest rum available in Hawai'i, won a gold medal in the Overproof Rum category at the American Distilling Institute's 2007 Rum Tasting Competition.

Based at Haleakalā Ranch in Upcountry Maui, the company is owned and operated by Jim and Leslie Sargent. A master distiller, Jim makes the rum in small batches with a dedicated eye to quality. He distills each batch twice in hand-wrought copper stills, ages them in American oak casks previously used for Jim Beam bourbon and personally samples everything before releasing it for bottling.

Holding true to its commitment of giving back to the community, Haleakalā Distillers supports numerous organizations on Maui, including the Pacific Whale Foundation, Women Helping Women, Manao Radio (which is run entirely by volunteers) and Seabury Hall, an independent coed college-preparatory school in Makawao.

Hula Girl Beverages

P.O. Box 8010, Stockton, California 95208
(209) 483-4004
www.hulagirl.com

Although Hula Girl Beverages is based in California, the idea for it was hatched in Hawai'i. In November 2002, frequent Island visitors Billy and Lisa Shawver dined at Mama's Fish House on Maui. As they perused the cocktail menu, Trader Vic's Mai Tai caught their eye. No sooner had they begun sipping that legendary drink than an idea flashed through their minds on how they could fulfill their dream of living and working in Hawai'i.

They would sell bottled, ready-to-drink tropical cocktails that appealed to women. All the drinks would contain rum made with Hawaiian molasses. By the time they were eating dessert, they had outlined their business plan for Hula Girl Beverages.

Today, using rum made with molasses from Kaua'i's Gay & Robinson sugar plantation, a distillery in San Jose is producing four distinctive Hula Girl drinks, including the Moonlight Mai Tai. Once local distribution grows, the Shawvers vow Hawai'i will be home for both them and Hula Girl.

RumFire

Sheraton Waikīkī, 2255 Kalākaua Avenue, Honolulu, Hawai'i 96815
(808) 921-4600
www.rumfirewaikiki.com

With more than 100 brands of rum from Anguilla to Venezuela displayed in a 12-foot-high mahogany tower and available for tasting, RumFire is a hot spot for connoisseurs of premium libations. Its selection of rare vintage rums—the largest in the United States—includes Rhum Clement X.O., a blend of highly regarded Martinique rums dating back to 1952, 1970 and 1976.

Open for happy hour and dinner daily, RumFire offers an intriguing cocktail menu that includes The Tradewinds (see recipe on page 124). You also can sip straight rums by the glass. If you can't decide, order the sampler, composed of one-and-a-half-ounce servings of three different types of rum that change weekly.

Other draws: an oceanfront setting with a fabulous view of Diamond Head; a fun tapas menu (the Inside-Out Musubis, Fire-Grilled Mahimahi Tacos and Seared Kālua Pulled Pork Quesadillas are standouts); and eight fire pits, five set in two outdoor seating areas that can be reserved for private parties.

Origin of
the Mai Tai

Although the mai tai has become as much a symbol of Hawai'i as the hula, surfing and Diamond Head, it actually was born in California. That is certain. Beyond that, however, a bit of controversy arises.

One story anoints Donn Beach—a noted chef, world traveler and savvy businessman—as the creator of the world-famous cocktail. Another says the honor should be bestowed on Victor Bergeron, founder of the Trader Vic's restaurant empire, which now has more than 30 locations around the world, including Beijing, Berlin, Bangkok and Beirut.

Rivals who respected each other's accomplishments, Beach and Bergeron bickered about the origin of the mai tai for decades, and since both have passed away (Bergeron in 1984; Beach in 1989), the whole truth probably never will be known.

The closest to it might be the conclusion drawn by Tom Chapman, editor of *Spirit of Aloha*, the in-flight magazine for Aloha Airlines. In his article "The Sweet and Sour Saga of the Mai Tai," which appeared in the September/October 2006 issue, Chapman suggests both restaurateurs should be credited for the birth of the Aloha State's best-selling libation. Beach first came up with a rum drink that had "mai tai" in its name. His successful experiments with rum prompted Bergeron to conduct his own, which resulted in an entirely different cocktail called mai tai.

Here are both men's stories. Should they share the recognition? You be the judge.

Don the Beachcomber's Story

Ernest Raymond Beaumont Gantt was born in Mexia, Texas, but spent much of his early life on his grandfather's plantation just outside New Orleans. There, he acquired his mother's passion for cooking and, at her side, learned how to prepare the spicy Cajun food for which the region was known.

As he grew older, Gantt considered the world his home. A charming vagabond, he had a special affinity for warm climes; by 1932, when he was 24 years old, he had already visited Jamaica, the Marquesas, Papua New Guinea, Tahiti and Australia on his own.

In December of that year, Gantt took a break from his globe-trotting adventures and landed in Hollywood with a host of priceless expe-

Guests at the lavish lūʻau Beach hosted at Encino Plantation, his home in California, included some of Hollywood's biggest stars of the 1930s and 1940s—among them, Clark Gable, Vivien Leigh, Bing Crosby, Alice Faye and Gary Cooper.

riences under his belt, but very little money in his pockets. Often eating at soup kitchens, he parked cars, bootlegged whiskey, worked at Chinatown restaurants and did other odd jobs to make ends meet.

As luck would have it, Gantt discovered a modest diner called Simon's Cafeteria that served great meals for only a quarter. A few down-to-earth movie stars frequented the joint, including David Niven and Marlene Dietrich, whom he befriended. They opened the door to the movie industry for him, and he was hired as a technical adviser on several South Pacific-themed films over the ensuing years, including *Hell's Half Acre* (1954). Directors considered Gantt's knowledge of the region a valuable asset. They also admired his collection of artifacts, which often were used as set props. But this was not what would earn him a place in Hawaiian history.

In 1933, Gantt came across a 13-by-30-foot space on a street off Hollywood Boulevard that had been vacated by a tailor. He envisioned a tropical-themed hideaway filled with happy patrons in that cozy setting. Although there were no guarantees his idea would fly, he signed a five-year lease for $30 per month.

Gantt set up a bar with 30 stools and five small tables with chairs. He combed through his stash of souvenirs from his extensive travels and selected a variety of items—including seashells, wooden tikis, dried blowfish and parts of wrecked boats that he'd found on beaches—to decorate the place. Beside the front door, he hung a driftwood sign upon which was scrawled the words "Don's Beachcomber." Its specialties were original tropical drinks and Chinese dishes that appealed to American palates.

The cocktail menu, which changed at Gantt's whim, was handwritten on a board behind the bar.

With Prohibition just repealed, he was free to serve all kinds of libations, most of which were based on the 140 rums from 16 different countries, including Cuba and Haiti, that were stored in his rum cellar at the restaurant. Gantt often went on buying trips to the Caribbean, where he would sample rum after rum and bring back two-year supplies of the ones he liked best. He loved to experiment with flavors and created more than 90 rum drinks in the 1930s and 1940s, among them a robust after-dinner concoction called the Mai Tai Swizzle. Ironically, this 1933 creation wasn't his personal favorite, but it was to become his best known.

Gantt was as well liked as his drinks, which no doubt was the reason why Don's Beachcomber quickly became a hangout for Hollywood's elite. Movie stars and top studio executives stopped by regularly. No one, it seemed, could have just one of Gantt's irresistible drinks.

A well-dressed gentleman once sauntered in and sipped a Sumatra Kula. Declaring it the best drink he'd had in a while, he ordered another, then another. He introduced himself as Neil Vanderbilt, a reporter for the New York Tribune, and on his next visit he brought friends with him, including Charlie Chaplin.

Beach opened a new Don the Beachcomber restaurant at the International Market Place in 1955. Perched among the branches of a banyan tree, it was in operation until the 1960s.

By 1937, it was obvious Don's Beachcomber had outgrown its small space, so Gantt moved it to a larger location in Hollywood and decorated it, like its predecessor, with a plethora of Polynesian kitsch. So much a part of his life had the business become, he legally changed his name to Donn Beach, but thereafter many people knew him by his nickname—Don the Beachcomber.

Travel remained Beach's other passion. He first visited Hawai'i in 1922, and made numerous return trips until he decided to make a permanent move there in 1946. By then, he was known as the premier developer of the "tiki bar" and Polynesian-themed restaurants and nightclubs, and in 1947, he opened Don the Beachcomber—three Polynesian-style longhouses set amid palm and banyan trees—on the property where Macy's now stands in Waikīkī.

Crowds packed the place, the big draws including top entertainers such as pianist Martin Denny, singer Alfred Apaka and hula dancer 'Iolani Luahine; a casual ambience, complete with Beach's trademark array of tropical mementos; and an enticing menu of exotic rum drinks and cuisine.

Not one to rest on his laurels, Beach teamed up with architect Pete Wimberly to design and develop the International Market Place on an adjacent parcel. That still-popular shopping and dining complex opened in 1955, with a new Don the Beachcomber perched in the branches of a spreading banyan (the original restaurant was torn down). Beach's successful Polynesian theme was again evident here in the décor, food and cocktails, including his scintillating Mai Tai Swizzle (he later shortened the drink's name to Mai Tai).

Postcards and matchbooks from Don the Beachcomber made great Hawai'i souvenirs.

Many of the rums used for Beach's concoctions are no longer being made, so here is his Original Mai Tai recipe with recommended substitutions, courtesy of his widow, Phoebe Beach, and her husband Arnold Bitner.

The Original Mai Tai

Into a mixer pour:

1½ oz.	Myers's Plantation rum*
1 oz.	Cuban rum
¾ oz.	fresh lime juice
1 oz.	fresh grapefruit juice
¼ oz.	Falernum
½ oz.	Cointreau
2	dashes of Angostura bitters
	Dash of Pernod
	Shell of squeezed lime
1 c.	cracked ice (size of a dime)

Shake for one minute at medium speed. Serve in a double old-fashioned glass. Garnish with four sprigs of mint. Add a spear of pineapple. Sip slowly through mint sprigs until desired effect results.

* Recommended rum substitutions: 1½ oz. Appleton Estate or 1 oz. British Navy-style rum such as Pusser's or Lamb's.

Trader Vic's Story

The son of an Oakland grocer, Victor Jules Bergeron, Jr. was destined to find success in the food business. His family lived in an apartment above their store, and from the time he was young, he played a hands-on role in the venture, from stocking shelves and doing inventory to mopping floors and running the cash register. Even at that tender age, Bergeron was a colorful character known for his mischievous deeds and his penchant for storytelling.

When he was about six years old, he fell off the roof of a backyard shed at home and broke his left leg. Reset three times, the leg developed gangrene and had to be amputated, but that never hindered him. In 1932, at the age of 30, Bergeron built a little pub across the street from his family's store with $700 in savings and carpentry help from his wife Esther's brothers.

Right: **Hinky Dinks, Bergeron's first restaurant, was known for its Eskimo artifacts and simple, hearty fare.**

Above: **When he renamed the eatery Trader Vic's, he changed the décor, food and cocktail menu to follow the new Polynesian theme.**

Dubbed Hinky Dinks after the catchy World War I song "Hinky Dinky Parlez Vous," it was decorated with snowshoes, bear skins and other Eskimo memorabilia. It soon became one of the most popular gathering spots in the Bay Area, known as much for its scampish owner as its nickel beers and hearty 25-cent meals of oxtail stew, roast chicken and lamb cheeks. Esther cooked while Bergeron tended the bar.

In 1934, the couple took a month-long vacation to Louisiana, Trinidad and Cuba, in part for rest and recreation, in part for research. Interested in finding novel cocktails that could be added to Hinky Dinks' menu, they sampled hurricanes in New Orleans, rum punch in Port of Spain and daiquiris in Havana.

During their travels, a lightbulb clicked on in Bergeron's head about how he could reinvent himself and his business. When he returned to California, he checked out South Seas, a new tropical-themed restaurant in San Francisco, and a similar establishment in Los Angeles called Don's Beachcomber. Inspired by what he saw, he began thinking about how he could add his own unique touch to their models.

First, Bergeron realized the name Hinky Dinks had to go. Because he was always wheeling and dealing, Esther suggested Trader Vic's. He loved it and even spun a tall tale to go along with the new name. With a straight face, he would tell customers he had lost his leg to a shark while swimming in the Pacific, and for dramatic effect, he'd grab an ice pick and jab it into his peg leg.

Crowds gathered at Trader Vic's nightly to enjoy food and fun with a Polynesian flair. Entertainment was provided by hula girls who easily persuaded patrons to join them for a dance or two.

Bergeron carried out the new theme with Polynesian food geared for American tastes and a décor of fishing nets, glass floats, rattan furniture, spears and such, some of which was reputedly purchased from Don the Beachcomber. Esteemed *San Francisco Chronicle* columnist Herb Caen, a regular guest, paid Trader Vic's the ultimate compliment in 1936 when he wrote "the best restaurant in San Francisco is in Oakland."

All the while, Bergeron was having a grand time concocting cocktails that, like Trader Vic's food and embellishments, stirred up exotic images of Polynesia. Sometime in 1944, he was at the restaurant's bar and took down a bottle of 17-year-old J. Wray Nephew Rum from Jamaica. Knowing the best cocktail recipes often were the simplest ones and that the rum's intense taste shouldn't be overpowered with too many flavorings, he added the juice of a lime, a bit of orange curacao from Holland, a splash of French orgeat, a dash of rock candy syrup and plenty of shaved ice. After vigorously shaking the drink, he poured it into two 15-ounce glasses, garnished each of them with half of the lime shell and a sprig of fresh mint, and served them to Eastham and Carrie Guild, good friends from Tahiti who happened to be in the restaurant that night.

Bergeron was an avid mixologist, which, according to one story, is how the mai tai was born.

In Bergeron's words, "Carrie took one sip and said, *Mai Tai—Roa Ae!* In Tahitian this means 'Out of This World—The Best!' Well, that was that. I named the drink 'Mai Tai.'"

The drink was an instant success not only in Oakland, but at Trader Vic's second location in Seattle, which opened in 1948. Five years later, Bergeron took the mai tai to Hawai'i, where Matson Steamship Lines had asked him to create drinks for its Royal Hawaiian, Moana and Surfrider hotels. As the story goes, Bergeron introduced 10 drinks, including the mai tai, at

Drink in hand (albeit not a mai tai), Bergeron celebrated the success of Trader Vic's on a relaxing cruise.

the Royal Hawaiian. It was the hands-down favorite, and within a month, customers were ignoring the other nine.

Mai tai fever caught on, and other local bars started serving their own interpretations of it. Meanwhile, by the early 1960s, Bergeron's mai tai became the most popular offering not only at Matson's hotels in Hawai'i, but at the 20 Trader Vic's restaurants in the United States at that time. Over the years, however, the recipe has been adjusted three times due to dwindling availability of its original ingredients.

Trader Vic's current mai tai recipe includes its own flavoring mix and dark rum—a blend of Jamaican, Martinique and Virgin Island rums that purportedly captures the smooth, nut-like characteristics of the 17-year-old J. Wray Nephew Rum. That recipe is shared here, along with The Original Formula, courtesy of Trader Vic's Inc.

The Original Mai Tai Formula

2 oz.   17-year-old J. Wray Nephew Rum
½ oz.   French Garnier Orgeat
½ oz.   Holland DeKuyper Orange Curacao
¼ oz.   rock candy syrup
       Juice of one fresh lime

Hand shake and garnish with half of the lime shell inside the drink. Float a sprig of fresh mint at the edge of the glass.

Present-Day Formula

2 oz.   fine dark rum
4 oz.   Trader Vic's Mai Tai Mix
       Juice of one large lime

Mai Tai Tales

For many, "mai tai" conjures up unforgettable memories of Hawai'i. Here are a few favorites from former and current Island residents.

Unraveling the Mystery of the Mai Tai

Late in 2003, a professional mixologist named Jamin Margeretich, then working at a place in Kona on the Big Island called Korner Pocket, got me involved in the saga of the mai tai when he won The Search for Hawai'i's Greatest Bacardi Mai Tai. His concoction, called an Easter Island Mai Tai, outlasted some 50 other entries and was judged superior based on points awarded for taste, appearance and presentation. Margeretich's winning cocktail was served in the face of a Pacific chief carved from a pineapple. His advice for making a great mai tai was "to drink a lot of them first."

In my account of this event, I wrote in what I considered to be an innocuous aside that "nobody knows for sure who created the first mai tai." I should have added that, regarding its provenance, there is much mystery and almost no agreement.

Two weeks later, an e-mail arrived from a public relations operative representing Trader Vic's, the legendary purveyor of Polynesian-themed

food, drinks and faux fantasy. "We were very surprised," said the message, more or less, "that you are misinformed about the origins of the mai tai, since it is well known, and has been well documented for many years, that this classic drink was invented by Vic Bergeron, the founder of Trader Vic's." And so forth. On the whole, it was a very friendly, but forthright message, and it concluded by inviting me, the next time I was in the Bay Area, which is where Trader Vic's is headquartered, to drop by for an authentic and, thus, by virtue of its authenticity, a historic mai tai, made the way it ought to be, had been for many years and still was, thank you, at Trader Vic's.

True to his word, when I showed up in San Francisco, Hans Richter, [then] president and chief executive officer of Trader Vic's Inc., bought me a mai tai. In fact, he bought me two mai tais: one made from the Second Adjusted Mai Tai Formula, the other made from the popular Trader Vic's Mai Tai Mix. He even watched closely while his bartender, Jim Shoemake, carefully followed the recipes.

I asked Richter, an unassuming, affable gentleman, who was hired by Vic Bergeron in 1969, why he works so hard to keep the legend of the mai tai alive. He said it was very important, because the mai tai is still the most popular drink at Trader Vic's, and, for that matter, throughout the tropics. "It is not a matter of whether Vic created the story afterwards or out of nowhere. It is important to know that we're still probably the only bar in the world where everything is fresh, natural and measured. Trader Vic's bartenders still get up to six months' training, so they know what they're doing. With all the different flavors and ingredients of a good mai tai, it's a tough assignment to keep up with the legend. And, by the way, please make a note that we never put paper umbrellas in our drinks, although everybody always claimed we did."

—Tom Chapman, Honolulu, O'ahu, excerpted from "The Sweet and Sour Saga of the Mai Tai," Spirit of Aloha (the in-flight magazine for Aloha Airlines), September/October 2006 issue

Rudy's Mai Tai

My close friend, Rudy Matthews, came to the United States from war-torn Germany many years ago. I don't know how he got to Hawai'i, but when I joined the Lutheran church in Kailua in 1967, there was Rudy.

My wife, Carol, and I enjoy playing bridge and we discovered that Rudy and his wife, Mary, also did, so it wasn't long before the four of us got together for cards and mai tais. We hadn't heard about Rudy's mai tai. Mary warned us that one is enough for most people.

When I first sipped it, I knew one was indeed plenty! Wow! What a zing! I asked Rudy if he would share his recipe. "Not a chance," he said.

Rudy, Mary, Carol and I got together for bridge and mai tais frequently over the ensuing years. Each time I had one of Rudy's mai tais. Each time I asked if I could have the recipe. The answer was always the same: a firm no.

Then as we were wrapping up one evening together, Rudy volunteered that he had put our names on his list in his will. "What list?" we asked. "The list of people who will get my mai tai recipe," he responded. We asked how many people were on the list. "Just three," he said.

I never asked for the recipe again. Twenty years later, Rudy died. After the funeral, Mary invited us to their home on the beach in Kailua. Family and friends from near and far arrived to celebrate Rudy's life. After the service, we gathered under a tent where food and a large pitcher had been set on a table.

Mary thanked everyone and finished by saying the pitcher was filled with Rudy's mai tai. "Just one," she said, "is enough for most people."

As the crowd dispersed into smaller groups, Mary sidled up to me and discreetly handed me a small sheet of paper, folded in half. "Rudy wanted you to have this," she said.

I didn't need to open it; I knew what it was. I thanked her (and Rudy) for being in our lives and for honoring us with his mai tai recipe.

We are normally beer and wine drinkers, but if some really special occasion is occurring and we can find all the ingredients, we will make Rudy's mai tai. When we do, we tell this story and add Mary's admonition—just one is enough for most people.

—*Larry Loose, Kailua, O'ahu*

The Trash Can Mai Tai

July 1983 marked my fourth Transpac race from Los Angeles to O'ahu. Six buddies and I sailed the 42-foot *Libalia Too* in that grueling 2,500-mile race, which biennially draws the finest competitors from all over the world.

Throughout our 10-day Pacific crossing, we took turns keeping watch, trimming the sails and taking the helm—tasks that tested our skills, knowledge, physical strength and intuition for we knew the ocean could be very unpredictable. The best part of every day was happy hour, just before sunset, because that was the only time all of us could gather on deck at once to relax and talk story.

Our libation of choice was a bottle of rum mixed with a pitcher of Tang, which we dubbed the Sailor's Mai Tai. Gourmets probably would turn up their noses at it, but out there in the open ocean at the end of a long day, with the wind and waves at our backs, we were certain no other drink could've tasted better.

When we crossed the finish line at Diamond Head, crews on greeting boats threw bottles of beer and champagne to us, but the best was yet to come. We anchored at Ala Wai Yacht Harbor and noticed a 35-gallon trash can on the dock. In it our friends and families had mixed several gallons of dark rum, several gallons of light rum, several quarts of passion-orange juice, dozens of pineapples and other fruits, and bags of ice into a giant mai tai that was topped off with a one-gallon float of Bacardi 151.

Party time! Our crew enjoyed generous portions of that Trash Can Mai Tai in hollowed-out pineapples, and other celebrants slipped in and out of the hot tub on one of the greeting boats with us, their own Trash Can Mai Tais in hand. Everybody had great fun—in fact, so much so it was amazing some of us were able to return to the boat the next day to clean up.

—*Rick McDonald, Kailua, O'ahu*

Clinking Glasses with Trader Vic

I moved to Honolulu from Fallbrook, Southern California (in San Diego County) in 1980 and immediately opened a jewelry store called The Rainbow Collection at Ala Moana Center. A group of older gentlemen who were customers of mine met regularly at the Mai Tai Bar at The Royal Hawaiian, and I joined them for a drink or two every now and then—always a mai tai. I really do love mai tais, and I'm rather picky about them!

Here's why: In the 1970s, I owned and operated three jewelry store and a tourmaline mining business in Southern California. An entrepreneur by the name of Victor Bergeron was a rock hound and quite a collector. He got wind of the mine and asked to tour it.

Turns out Mr. Bergeron was the gentleman of the "Trader Vic" fame! What fun my then-husband Bill Larson, and I had showing him the mine and subsequently visiting him at his San Francisco restaurant many times.

The first mai tai I ever tasted was mixed by the maestro himself and served in his private office (he worked at a giant desk made from a slab of a redwood tree). Vic was very proud of this mai tais and proclaimed that he was the originator of this now legendary drink!

Of course, his mai tai was fabulous and I've been hooked on the drink ever since. Cheers to my old and dear friend, Victor Bergeron, whom I miss very much!

I lived in Hawai'i for 25 years and always carry it in my heart.
—*Karla Proud, Bend, Oregon*

Love Story

Pretty, vivacious Barbara hailed from Seattle and was enjoying a winter vacation on Maui with her family.

Handsome, soft-spoken Ali had come to Maui from the Bay Area, seeking solace following the death of his mother.

Their paths crossed a decade ago at the Nāpili Kai Resort, where both befriended bartender Ricky Rickard.

One day, Barbara asked Ricky where she could meet eligible men on Maui. "Right here," said Ricky, thinking of Ali. "Come to happy hour at the Whalewatcher's Bar this afternoon."

When she did, Ricky introduced her to Ali. The two immediately hit it off, enjoying animated conversation over Ricky's refreshing mai tais. Not wanting the meeting to end, Barbara invited Ali to dinner with her family. At first, Ali declined, thinking it wouldn't be appropriate since he had just met her. But Ricky urged him to accept, saying, "Come on, you won't regret it."

Ali finally agreed to go, and Cupid's arrow found its mark. A year later, Ali and Barbara were married on the beach at Nāpili Bay with a gorgeous sunset as the backdrop. Most couples have a special song; Ali and Barbara have a special drink—the mai tai, of course, with which guests toasted them at their wedding reception.

Although the couple resides on the Mainland, Maui remains their favorite escape. Whenever they visit, they always have dinner at Nāpili Kai's Sea House restaurant and reserve time to sip mai tais and chat with Ricky at the Whalewatcher's Bar. Inevitably, they reminisce about the day they met and the role he played in their storybook romance.

—*Verna Biga, Kahana, Maui*

Nāpili Kai Resort, the romantic meeting place of Ali and Barbara.

Hawaiian-Style Welcome

In 1966, I was invited to sail in my first multihull Transpac race to Hawai'i aboard a 50-foot catamaran called *Glass Slipper*. At the time, multi-hulled vessels were not allowed to compete in the regular Transpac, which is held on odd-numbered years, so they competed in a separate event held during even-numbered years.

That also happened to be my first trip to Hawai'i. Some of the guys who built *Glass Slipper* with me had been to the Islands, and they would share wonderful stories about their visits as we worked. Needless to say, having been raised in California, I was looking forward to enjoying all the things I had heard about Hawai'i.

It took us 11 days to make the approximately 2,500-mile crossing from California, and I got my first glimpse of the Islands—Moloka'i, spe-cifically—as we approached the Kaiwi Channel. The view was utterly spec-tacular! We sailed through the channel in the mid-afternoon, rounding Koko Head and heading toward Diamond Head and the finish line with the sun bright and hot overhead.

When we crossed the finish line, we were told we should land *Glass Slipper* on the beach in front of the Outrigger Canoe Club, but there was one glitch: we wouldn't be able to disembark until inspectors from Hawai'i's Department of Agriculture gave us the green light. I'm not sure if it was planned or just a nice impromptu gesture by the Outrigger Canoe Club, but shortly afterward, milk cases were being handed to us over the bow of our boat. Instead of a milk bottle, however, each puka (hole) in the cases contained a mai tai!

Since there were no restrictions on who could come to our arrival party, we invited everyone on the beach to hop on board *Glass Slipper*, including a number of lovely ladies. In the company of new friends and with the sun setting over the ocean, tiki torches flickering on the beach, a warm breeze blowing and a mai tai in my hand, I remember thinking I could have received no better introduction to Hawai'i.

—Joe Cochran, Kāne'ohe, O'ahu

A Sip of Paradise

During an early morning breakfast on Kaua'i, three buddies and I heard our waiter, a local teen, telling a coworker that powerful south swells were slamming into the south and west shores. We hadn't a clue where to find them, so I did the unthinkable, at least by today's standards: I asked our waiter for directions.

To my surprise, he turned over a paper place mat and drew a map to a legendary spot south of Waimea. "The Hawaiian name is Pākalā," he said, "but it's also known as Infinities."

"Why Infinities?" I asked.

"Brah," he said, laughing, "the rides are so long your legs will be tired when you pull out."

By the time we raced back to our car, all four of us visiting surfers from California figured we were likely being led on a wild goose chase, but we decided to give it a shot. Following the map, we parked on the highway near an old bridge, then climbed a barbed wire fence and started walking down a narrow trail along a shallow, slow-moving stream.

We emerged on a beach 20 minutes later; the memory still gives me chicken skin. In front of us were the most perfect waves I had ever seen. From the point a half mile away, the three- to six-foot surf broke over a shallow reef into a picturesque cove. Only two other surfers were out. We immediately tossed our backpacks into the bushes and made a beeline for the water.

Five hours later, we dragged our sore and sated bodies onto shore, hungry but mostly thirsty. Someone said, "What I wouldn't give for a mai tai!"

"Yeah, me too," said my friend Steve, "so let's have one."

I laughed. "You gonna make a rum run?"

"No, you brought it," he replied. "Give me your backpack." He pulled out a bottle of dark Bacardi, two limes and a few plastic cups.

"Too bad you didn't put ice in someone's backpack," I said.

Steve leaned over to grab Danny's backpack. Inside was a bottle of mai tai mix and a block of ice wrapped in aluminum foil and two plastic bags. Out of Terry's backpack came a portable, battery-operated blender and a small bag of sliced pineapple.

We looked at each another and started laughing hysterically, rolling across fallen palm fronds, covering our bodies in wet sand, eyes tearing.

"I'll take care of this," said Steve. He blended everything, added the ice and voilà—mai tais!

By the time we finished drinking the concoction, we had relived our wave rides several times and made more toasts than I can remember to Bacardi, ex-girlfriends, current girlfriends, future girlfriends and, most of all, to Steve. Life was divine on this tiny patch of sand in the middle of the Pacific. No mai tais have ever tasted as good.

—Tim Ryan, Honolulu, O'ahu

A Bear Necessity

It was one of those rare hot summer days in Petersville, Alaska, which is about a two-hour drive north of Anchorage near Mount McKinley. My friend and I were sitting on the deck of his cabin there, enjoying mai tais after spending a full day of hard work building another cabin on the property.

Situated up a long dirt trail at the base of a mountain, this was a true "get-away-from-it-all" place with no running water or electricity. You had to drive 20 minutes through dense wilderness on either an ATV or snowmobile to get to it, and the nearest neighbor was three miles away.

We often saw black bears in the area, but seldom paid attention to them. That day, however, was different. We saw a big bear walking up the trail, lifting his head and sniffing the air as bears do.

He kept coming closer and closer; we were sure he saw us. Usually, bears leave when they spot humans, but not that bear, not that day. Realizing he was headed straight for us, we left our drinks on the deck and dashed into the cabin, securely locking the door behind us.

As we watched through a window, the bear walked onto the deck, sniffed around and found our mai tai pitcher. He overturned it and drank its contents, even licking drops off the deck! When he was done, he gave us a look of thanks and then slowly ambled down the trail. We can only assume he went to take a nice long nap. Needless to say, it was a most memorable Alaskan experience.

—Viktor Schmidt, Waikīkī, O'ahu

Lingering at the Longboard Bar

Before Lewers Street in Waikīkī was renovated with fancy new hotels, shops and dining establishments, there was a little watering hole at the Waikīkī Broiler restaurant called the Longboard Bar. With koa wood tables, hanging paper lanterns, the smell of salt air and "grass hula skirt" trim on the bar, it was a great example of Hawaiian kitsch.

The bar had a long, rich history, but I only discovered it a few years before it was demolished and replaced with buildings that had a lot more luster but, in my opinion, a lot less character. Its legal capacity was probably about 20 people, but on Friday nights three times that many would come to unwind over 99-cent mai tais.

Posted on a wall near the back of the bar, but visible from the street through a cloudy window, was a handpainted sign with these words scrawled in simple red letters: "99 Cent Mai Tais 6-9 p.m." I stumbled across it one Friday evening at about 7:15 p.m., smiled at my good fortune and went inside.

As usual, the place was packed. I worked my way through the crowd to a table near the bar and ordered two mai tais. They came in the kind of heavy six-ounce cola glasses that you would expect to find at a cheap buffet, yet they were poured perfectly. A beautiful dusty sunset rose from the bottom of each glass, and a fresh pineapple wedge, a bright maraschino cherry and a paper umbrella sat on their rims. Mai tai perfection!

I stayed at the bar long after the mai tai special ended, chatting with regulars and tourists alike, participated in a few rounds of karaoke and made a few friends. Wherever I was originally headed to that night didn't matter; I had found what I was looking for.

That summer in 2004, I was at the Longboard Bar almost every Friday night. You might say it was my summer of mai tais—a time to savor the carefree, innocent Hawai'i that now exists only in memories.

— *Maleko McDonnell, Kailua, O'ahu*

New-Wave
Mai Tai Recipes

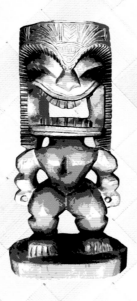

Mai Tai Shot

Cindy Goldstein

2¼ c. water
3-oz. package pineapple Jell-O
3-oz. package lemon Jell-O
¾ c. dark rum
¾ c. light rum
¼ c. triple sec

Boil water in saucepan. Turn off heat. Stir in pineapple and lemon Jell-O for at least a minute, until completely dissolved. Add rums and triple sec. Stir well. Pour into 32 one-ounce single-serve plastic cups using a measuring cup with a spout. Refrigerate cups for three to four hours. Yield: 32 one-ounce cups.

Tips: Don't use sugar-free Jell-O, and make sure the total amount of liquid is no more than half alcohol. If you use too much alcohol and less water, the shot will not set. It helps to loosen the shot by running a toothpick or your tongue all the way around the sides of the cup so you can get it out more easily. You don't "drink" this kind of shot; it is solid Jell-O, so you actually slurp it out of the cup. Serve chilled.

Cadillac Mai Tai

Embassy Suites - Waikīkī Beach Walk

½ oz. Bacardi Limón
½ oz. Malibu rum
 1 oz. mango purée
 1 oz. liliko'i purée
 1 oz. banana purée
 1 oz. coconut syrup
 2 oz. sweet-and-sour
 3 oz. pineapple juice
        Splash of Cointreau
        Splash of amaretto
        Splash of grenadine
 1 oz. Myers's rum

Pour first eight ingredients over ice in an exotic glass in the order listed. Blend them, then add Cointreau, amaretto and grenadine. Float Myers's rum. Garnish with a pineapple wedge and a maraschino cherry.

Fusion Mai Tai

Planet Hollywood Honolulu

¾ oz.   Grand Marnier
1½ oz.   Cointreau
1½ oz.   pineapple juice
1½ oz.   orange juice
¾ oz.   cabernet sauvignon

Fill 14-ounce highball glass with ice and pour in all ingredients but the wine. Pour into a shaker and shake for only about three seconds, until the juices mix together with the spirits. Pour mixed ingredients back into glass and float the wine. Garnish with an orchid and a pineapple wedge.

Buddha's Mai Tai

Doraku Sushi

1 oz. Bacardi Light Rum
1 oz. Myers's Dark Rum
½ oz. DeKuyper Apricot Liqueur
1 oz. liliko'i nectar
1 oz. lychee, puréed
½ oz. Coco Lopez
½ oz. pineapple juice
        Splash of grenadine

Shake all ingredients vigorously for ten seconds. Serve in a tiki mug or a 14-ounce highball glass over ice. Garnish with a sugarcane stick and a fresh lychee.

Very Berry Mai Tai

Kahala Hotel & Resort

½ oz. orgeat
½ oz. simple syrup
1¼ oz. lemon juice, freshly squeezed
1½ oz. fresh pineapple juice
 1 oz. Bacardi Silver Rum
½ oz. Cointreau
1¼ oz. blueberry preserves
 1 oz. Coruba rum

Add the first six ingredients to a shaker with ice. Shake and chill. Add blueberry preserves. Muddle in the shaker until all ingredients are mixed. Pour into a glass with ice (you can strain the drink into the glass if you like). Float rum. Garnish with an orchid and a pineapple wedge.

Frozen Mai Tai

Keoki's Paradise

16 oz. ice
½ oz. Bacardi 151 Rum
2 oz. POG (passion-orange-guava juice)
2 oz. passion sherbet
½ oz. dark rum

Blend first four ingredients until smooth. Pour into a glass or a tiki mug and top with dark rum. Garnish with a pineapple wedge and a paper parasol.

Grand Mai Tai

Grand Wailea Resort Hotel & Spa

1 ¼ oz. Grand Marnier
  1 oz. dark rum
 ½ oz. pineapple juice, freshly squeezed
 ½ oz. orange juice, freshly squeezed
   3 lime wedges, squeezed

Shake all ingredients and pour into a glass over coarsely crushed ice. Garnish with a pineapple wedge, an orange wedge and an orchid.

Hana Hou Mai Tai

Duke's Kaua'i,
Kaua'i Marriott Resort & Beach Club

5   fresh mint leaves
2   splashes of POG
     (passion-orange-guava juice)
½ oz. Malibu rum
¼ oz. liliko'i syrup
1 oz. dark rum

Muddle mint leaves and add to POG, Malibu rum and liliko'i syrup in a shaker. Shake well. Strain and pour into a 13-ounce glass over ice. Float dark rum. Garnish with a maraschino cherry, a lime wedge and a sprig of mint.

LuLu's Specialty Mai Tai

LuLu's Surf Club Waikīkī Beach

1½ oz. guava juice
1½ oz. pineapple juice
1½ oz. orange juice
  1 oz. mango purée
½ oz. Diamond Head 151 Rum
½ oz. Captain Morgan Spiced Rum
½ oz. Myers's Dark Rum
½ oz. Diamond Head Dark Rum

Mix juices and mango purée. Fill a 12-ounce glass with ice. Pour in 151 rum and spiced rum. Pour in the fruit mix. Float two dark rums. Garnish with a pineapple wedge, a maraschino cherry, a slice of lime and an orchid.

Maui Mai Tai

Haleakalā Distillers

½ oz.   Maui Platinum Rum
½ oz.   Maui Gold Rum
½ oz.   Braddah Kimo's Extreme 155 Rum
         Juice from one lime
         Splash of pomegranate juice
½ oz.   orange curaçao
3 Tbsp. Sugar in the Raw turbinado sugar
½ oz.   orgeat
½ oz.   Maui Dark Rum

Pour first three ingredients in a glass over shaved ice. Add lime and pomegranate juices. Add orange curaçao, raw sugar and orgeat. Shake vigorously. Pour into a cored pineapple. Float dark rum. Garnish with a lime wedge and a paper parasol.

Caution: This is a very strong four-rum cocktail. Please enjoy in moderation.

Hard Rocker Mai Tai

Hard Rock Cafe Honolulu

1 oz.	Chambord
3 oz.	pineapple juice
3 oz.	orange juice
1½ oz.	light rum
1 oz.	Myers's Dark Rum

Fill 20-ounce glass with ice. Pour in Chambord. Add pineapple and orange juices. Add light rum. Float dark rum. Garnish with a pineapple wedge and a maraschino cherry.

Kahuwai Mai Tai

Kona Village Resort

¾ oz. Cruzan Estate Dark Rum
½ oz. peach schnapps
½ oz. triple sec
 1 oz. sweet-and-sour
 2 oz. pineapple juice
 1 oz. orange juice
       Splash of Myers's Dark Rum

Fill a 12-ounce glass with ice. Pour all ingredients, except the Myers's Dark Rum, into the glass and stir. Float Myers's Dark Rum.

Kūhiō Delight

Hilton Waikīkī Prince Kūhiō Hotel

¼ oz.   orgeat
½ oz.   Bacardi Silver Rum
½ oz.   Bacardi Gold Rum
½ oz.   Cointreau
½ oz.   Mandarin Napoleon
       Splash of apple juice
       Splash of orange juice
       Splash of pineapple juice
½ oz.   Gosling's rum

Mix all ingredients, except for the Gosling's rum, and shake well. Float Gosling's rum. Garnish with pineapple and lime wedges.

Mai Tai Royal

Halekūlani, On the Beach at Waikīkī

¾ oz. añejo rum
½ oz. orange curaçao
1 oz. orgeat
¼ oz. fresh lime juice
3 oz. champagne

Pour the first four ingredients in a Boston shaker glass with ice cubes. Pour champagne slowly over the ice while gently dragging the ingredients up from the bottom of the glass to avoid losing the bubbles. Strain into a champagne flute and serve. Garnish with a flamed orange peel and an orchid.

Thai Tai

Hukilau Lānai, Kaua'i Coast Resort

¾ oz. Hawaiian Vanilla-Infused
       Spiced Rum
       Splash of Ginger Basil Syrup
3 oz. pineapple juice
3 oz. sweet-and-sour
¼ oz. dark rum
       Squeeze of lime

Pack 14-ounce glass with ice and pour in first five ingredients in the order listed. Float dark rum and add lime. Garnish with a sprig of basil and a slice of candied ginger.

Hawaiian Vanilla-Infused Spiced Rum
Slit two Hawai'i-grown vanilla beans down the center and pry open. Place beans in bottle of spiced rum and soak for two days.

Ginger Basil Syrup

2 c. sugar
3 c. water
2 oz. ginger root, peeled and sliced
1 oz. Thai basil
¼ c. fresh lemon juice

Combine all ingredients in a medium saucepan and bring to a boil. Turn off heat and steep for fifteen minutes. Cool and strain. Yield: About three cups.

Sassy Wahine

Pineapple Grill

1 oz.	Bacardi Light Rum
½ oz.	orange curaçao
½ oz.	Gingered Orgeat
2 oz.	pineapple juice
2 oz.	guava juice
½ oz.	Whaler's Dark Rum
¼ oz.	Bacardi 151 Rum

In order, pour light rum, orange curaçao, Gingered Orgeat and juices into a tulip glass filled with ice. Float dark rum and splash 151 rum on top. Serve unstirred. Garnish with a lime wheel and a pineapple wedge.

Gingered Orgeat

1	piece of fresh ginger, thumb-size
1 c.	orgeat
½ c.	fresh lime juice
1 c.	fresh mint, loosely packed

Smash ginger and place in a saucepan with orgeat and lime juice. Warm over medium heat until mixture just bubbles around edges of pan. Add fresh mint and stir for five minutes. Strain through a fine sieve and cool. Keep refrigerated.

Paradise Found Mai Tai

Don's Mai Tai Bar, Royal Kona Resort

½ oz. mango rum
½ oz. coconut rum
½ oz. pineapple rum
½ oz. orgeat
      Pineapple juice as needed
      Splash of lemon-lime soda

Mix rums and orgeat in a 10-ounce glass filled with ice. Add pineapple juice almost to the top of the glass (leave about half an inch "open"). Top with soda. Garnish with a pineapple slice, a maraschino cherry and a paper parasol.

Nightlife Mai Tai

Donna Jung
A tribute to "Mr. Hawai'i," Don Ho

1½ oz. light rum
1½ oz. orange curaçao
 1 oz. pineapple juice
 1 oz. unsweetened liliko'i juice
1½ oz. crème de cassis
 ½ oz. dark rum

Fill a large shaker three-fourths full of ice. Add light rum, orange curaçao, and pineapple and liliko'i juices. Shake vigorously. Fill mai tai glass with ice and pour the crème de cassis in it to create the first layer. Slowly pour the earlier shaken mixture into the glass using a pouring screen; this will create a second layer. Finish by gently pouring the dark rum on top to create the third layer. The three separate layers should now be distinct: the bottom layer should be purple, the middle amber and the top a warm brown. Garnish with a three-inch heart of sugarcane stick, three frozen black currants and a sprig of mint.

Take-Off Mai Tai

Duke's Kaua'i,
Kaua'i Marriott Resort & Beach Club

1 oz.	Captain Morgan rum
½ oz.	Malibu rum
3 oz.	pineapple juice
	Splash of liliko'i syrup
	Pinch of li hing mui powder
4	squeezes of lime or a few splashes of Rose's lime juice
½ oz.	amaretto
½ oz.	Grand Marnier

Shake first six ingredients and pour in a glass over ice. Float amaretto and Grand Marnier. Garnish with a pineapple wedge dipped in li hing mui powder.

The Kiss

Matthew Gray

1 oz. rum
1 oz. spiced rum
1 oz. pomegranate juice
1 oz. orange juice
2 oz. pineapple juice
¼ oz. grenadine
1 oz. ginger ale
½ oz. dark rum

Pour rum and spiced rum in glass over ice. Top with juices, grenadine and ginger ale. Float dark rum. Garnish with a maraschino cherry, a peeled stick of ginger and a pineapple wedge.

Mai Tai-Jito

Duke's Waikīkī,
Outrigger Waikīkī on the Beach

In a mixing tin, muddle:

6 to 8	fresh mint leaves
5 to 6	chunks fresh pineapple
4 to 5	fresh lime wedges
1 Tbsp.	raw sugar
2 tsp.	candied ginger
1 tsp.	mango purée

Then add:

1 oz.	Myers's rum
¾ oz.	Bacardi White Rum
1 oz.	pineapple juice
1 oz.	liliko'i juice
1 oz.	guava juice
½ oz.	Captain Morgan Spiced Rum

Rim a large martini glass with more raw sugar and/or candied ginger. Add ice to the mixing tin, shake well and strain into the glass. Float spiced rum. Garnish with a lime wedge.

Mmm' Aloha Tai

Hukilau Sports Bar & Grill

1 oz.	strawberry purée
6 to 8	mint leaves
4 to 6	strawberries, sliced
1 oz.	mango rum
½ oz.	coconut rum
1 oz.	pineapple juice
1 oz.	sour mix
	Splash of 7-UP or Sprite
½ oz.	dark rum

Pour strawberry purée in a 14-ounce glass. In a shaker, put in the mint leaves, sliced strawberries, mango rum, coconut rum, pineapple juice, sour mix and soda. Gently shake until all ingredients are combined. Add contents of the shaker into the glass, being careful to pour it along the side so that the purée isn't disturbed. Float with dark rum and garnish with a fanned strawberry and mint leaf.

Notes: If a sugared rim is desired, do this prior to pouring the drink. Stir cocktail prior to drinking.

Mount Ka'ala Mai Tai

Sansei Seafood Restaurant & Sushi Bar,
Waikīkī Beach Marriott Resort & Spa

3 to 4   sprigs of mint
1 ¼ oz.   Mount Gay Eclipse Rum
½ oz.   Cointreau
1 ½ oz.   fresh pineapple juice
1 ½ oz.   fresh orange juice
½ oz.   liliko'i concentrate
¼ oz.   orgeat
      Myers's Dark Rum as needed
      Splash of Lemon Hart 151

Twist mint sprigs to release their oils and put in a shaker tin. Fill the shaker with ice. Add the Mount Gay rum, Cointreau, pineapple and orange juices, liliko'i concentrate and orgeat. Shake vigorously to mix all ingredients well and pour into a hurricane glass. Float the Myers's rum, then splash the Lemon Hart 151 on top. Garnish with a sprig of mint, a fresh pineapple slice and an orange flag (thin orange wedge wrapped around a maraschino cherry with a cocktail pick).

Silky Mai Thai

Chai's Island Bistro

¾ oz. amaretto
¾ oz. Southern Comfort
¾ oz. Midori
½ oz. gin
½ oz. grenadine
 1 oz. sweet-and-sour
¾ oz. dark rum
        Pineapple juice as needed

Fill a 12- to 15-ounce glass with ice cubes. Pour all ingredients, except pineapple juice and rum, in the order listed. Fill rest of glass with pineapple juice and top with rum. Garnish with an orchid, a maraschino cherry and a pineapple wedge.

Pineapple and Mango
Rum Cocktail

Maui Pineapple Co.

2½   small ripe mangoes, peeled and
       cubed (about 2 cups)
4 oz. golden rum
½ c. water
4 c. fresh pineapple juice
       (about the amount obtained
       from a 4½-pound pineapple)

Purée mangoes, rum and water in a blender. Pour two ounces of purée into each of six 12-ounce glasses. Fill glasses with ice and top off with pineapple juice. Garnish with slices of fresh mango and star fruit. Yield: Six 12-ounce drinks.

Upside-Down Mai Tai-Tini

Planet Hollywood Honolulu

½ oz. Absolut Pear Vodka
1 ½ oz. Bacardi Razz Rum
½ oz. DeKuyper Tropical Pineapple
           Splash of 7-UP
½ oz. Chambord

Mix vodka, rum, Tropical Pineapple and 7-UP with ice. Strain into a chilled martini glass. Slowly pour Chambord on side of glass until it reaches the bottom (this will give the drink a layered upside-down look). Garnish with a pineapple wedge.

Mango Mai Tai

ResortQuest Islander on the Beach

1 oz.	Diamond Head White Rum
1 oz.	Maui Mango
	(Maui Ice Co. mango purée)
2½ oz.	orange juice
2½ oz.	pineapple juice
	Splash of orange curaçao
2	drops of orgeat
1 oz.	Myers's Dark Rum
	Lime wedge

Pour all ingredients, except the dark rum and lime, in a 14-ounce glass filled with ice. Float dark rum. Add squeeze of juice from the lime. Garnish with the lime wedge, a maraschino cherry, a pineapple wedge and a paper parasol.

Mai Maui Tai

Aloha Mixed Plate

1 oz.	light rum
1 oz.	Malibu Pineapple Rum
1 oz.	Jim Beam
½ oz.	Chambord
½ oz.	banana liqueur
2 oz.	orange juice
2 oz.	pineapple juice
	Splash of grenadine

Shake all ingredients with ice and pour in an exotic glass.
Garnish with a pineapple slice and a sugarcane stick.

Mary's Memorable Mai Tai

Lahaina Grill

Li hing mui powder
½ oz. orange curaçao
½ oz. Bacardi Light Rum
½ oz. peach schnapps
2 oz. pineapple juice
½ oz. mango purée
1 oz. Hana Bay Dark Rum
Lime wedge

Rim glass with li hing mui powder. Pour all ingredients, except the lime wedge, in a glass filled with ice in the order listed. Add squeeze of lime juice. Garnish with the lime wedge, a sprig of mint and a maraschino cherry.

Amarango Mai Tai

Four Seasons Resort Huālalai

1 oz. Mount Gay Mango Rum
1 oz. sweet-and-sour
1 oz. Amaretto Disaronno
2 oz. pineapple juice
½ oz. mango purée
¾ oz. Myers's Dark Rum

Pour all ingredients, except the dark rum, into a glass in the order listed. Float dark rum. Garnish with a pineapple wedge, a lime wedge and a miniature orchid.

Wiki Wiki Mango Mai Tai

Mauna Kea Resort

  1 oz. Bacardi Light Rum
½ oz. orange curaçao
½ oz. orgeat
½ oz. simple syrup
  2 oz. lime juice
  2 oz. mango purée
  1 oz. Myers's Dark Rum

Fill 18-ounce English highball glass with crushed ice. Pour all ingredients, except the dark rum, into the glass. Float dark rum. Garnish with a pineapple wedge, a maraschino cherry, a sprig of mint and a vanda orchid.

Upside-Down
Fruit Stand Mai Tai

JW Marriott Ihilani Resort & Spa

½ oz.   Kona coffee liqueur
½ oz.   banana liqueur
½ oz.   Kahana Royale Macadamia Nut
      Liqueur
¾ oz.   Malibu Coconut Rum
1 oz.   pineapple juice
1   lime, squeezed

Coat rim of a mai tai glass with finely chopped toasted sweetened coconut. Fill glass with ice. Pour ingredients into glass in the order listed. Garnish with a pineapple wedge and an orchid.

Mai-tini

Ruth's Chris Steak House, Honolulu

½ oz. Bacardi White Rum
¼ oz. Grand Marnier
¼ oz. Peachtree Peach Schnapps
2½ oz. POG (passion-orange-guava juice)
½ oz. Myers's Dark Rum
      Splash of grenadine
1 lime wedge
½ oz. Hana Bay Dark Rum

Fill a martini shaker with ice. Add all ingredients, except the lime and Hana Bay rum. Squeeze juice from lime in the shaker. Shake vigorously and pour into a chilled martini glass. Float the Hana Bay rum. Drop a purple vanda orchid into the glass and garnish with a pineapple slice.

Makawao Mai Tai

OCEAN Vodka

1 oz. OCEAN Vodka
2 oz. pineapple juice
        Splash of fresh orange juice
        Splash of Whaler's Dark Rum

Pour vodka and pineapple and orange juices over ice in
your favorite cocktail glass. Top with dark rum. Garnish
with fresh fruit of your choice and a paper parasol.

Mai Tai Royale

Hilton Hawaiian Village Beach Resort & Spa

2 oz. pineapple juice
2 oz. lime juice
1 oz. Bacardi rum
½ oz. Grand Marnier
½ oz. amaretto
1 oz. Myers's rum

Fill glass with ice and add pineapple and lime juices. Add Bacardi rum, Grand Marnier and amaretto. Float Myers's rum. Do not stir or shake! Garnish with a pineapple wedge and an orchid.

Prince Special

Hilton Waikīkī Prince Kūhiō Hotel

1 oz.	Bacardi Gold Rum
1 oz.	Soho Lychee
1 oz.	Malibu Mango Rum
1 oz.	pineapple juice
1 oz.	orange juice
	Splash of grenadine
½ oz.	dark rum

Mix all ingredients, except for the dark rum, and shake well. Float dark rum. Garnish with pineapple and lime wedges.

PJ's Magic Mai Tai

Anna Nordin

1½ oz. Bacardi Gold Rum
  1 oz. Captain Morgan Spiced Rum
  1 oz. Malibu rum
  1 oz. Myers's Dark Rum
  ½ oz. banana liqueur
  1 oz. guava juice
        Splash of orange juice
        Splash of pineapple juice

Pour ingredients in a shaker with four to six ice cubes and shake vigorously. Pour drink into a glass. Garnish with a pineapple wedge and a sprig of mint.

Lava Love

CanoeHouse, Mauna Lani Resort

	Crushed rock candy
1½ oz.	Malibu Pineapple Rum
½ oz.	Bacardi rum
¼ oz.	Chambord
¾ oz.	guava juice
	Dash of grenadine

Rim glass with crushed rock candy. Mix ingredients and pour drink into glass. Garnish with a sprig of mint.

Pakini Mai Tini

Embassy Suites - Waikīkī Beach Walk

	Lemon wedge
1 Tbsp.	sugar
1 ¼ oz.	Jose Cuervo Oranjo Tequila
2 oz.	passion-orange juice
¼ oz.	dark rum

Rub lemon wedge around the rim of a martini glass. Put sugar in a saucer and run the rim of the glass through it to coat it. Mix tequila and passion-orange juice in a shaker. Shake and strain into the glass. Float dark rum. Sink a maraschino cherry as the garnish.

Piña Colada Shot

Cindy Goldstein

　1 c.　water
3-oz.　package pineapple Jell-O
　¾ c.　coconut rum
　¼ c.　light rum

Boil water in a saucepan. Turn off heat. Stir in pineapple Jell-O for at least one minute, until completely dissolved. Add rums. Stir well. Pour into 16 one-ounce, single-serve plastic cups using a measuring cup with a spout. Refrigerate cups for three to four hours. Yield: 16 one-ounce cups.

Tips: Don't use sugar-free Jell-O, and make sure the total amount of liquid is no more than half alcohol. If you use too much alcohol and less water, the shot will not set. It helps to loosen the shot by running a toothpick or your tongue all the way around the sides of the cup so you can get it out more easily. You don't "drink" this kind of shot; it is solid Jell-O, so you actually slurp it out of the cup. Serve chilled.

Majestic Mai Tai

Beach House Restaurant

1¼ oz.	Malibu Coconut Rum
1 Tbsp.	mango purée
1 Tbsp.	passion fruit syrup
1 Tbsp.	orgeat
1 Tbsp.	orange juice
1 Tbsp.	sweet-and-sour
	Pineapple juice as needed
1 oz.	Bacardi 151 Rum
1 oz.	Myers's Dark Rum
	Dash of grenadine

Pour coconut rum into a 16-ounce glass that's three-fourths full of ice. Add mango purée, passion fruit syrup, orgeat, orange juice, and sweet-and-sour. Add pineapple juice until drink is approximately one inch from the top of the glass. Shake vigorously. Fill the remainder of the glass with crushed ice. Float 151 rum, dark rum and grenadine. Garnish with two pineapple leaves and a maraschino cherry speared on a pineapple wedge.

Wai'alae Mai Tai

3660 on the Rise

2	whole strawberries
2	lychees, seed removed
1 oz.	lychee syrup
1 oz.	pineapple juice
¾ oz.	limeade
	Squeeze of lime and lemon juice
½ oz.	coconut syrup
1 oz.	10 Cane Rum
½ oz.	Malibu rum
½ oz.	Bacardi Limón
½ oz.	orange curaçao
1 oz.	Myers's Dark Rum

Muddle the strawberries and lychees in a glass. Add the rest of the ingredients, except the dark rum. Float dark rum. Garnish with a maraschino cherry and an orange slice.

Lēʻahi

Chuck's Steak House,
Outrigger Waikīkī on the Beach

1 oz.   Captain Morgan Spiced Rum
½ oz. orange curaçao
1 oz.   lilikoʻi juice
1 oz.   cranberry juice
¼ oz. mango purée
1 oz.   Diamond Head Dark Rum

Mix all ingredients in a 14-ounce glass. Fill remainder of glass with ice. Garnish with pineapple and lime wedges.

Mai Tai Roa Ae

Alan Wong's Restaurant

This specialty drink is a three-part recipe: the sorbet syrup, the falernum (four days to macerate) and the mixed drink.

Sorbet Syrup

  1 pt. water
4½ c. granulated sugar
  1 pt. corn syrup

Mix water and sugar at room temperature until all the sugar has dissolved. Add corn syrup and mix thoroughly. Heat the mixture over medium heat until it reaches the boiling point. Reduce the heat to low and simmer for five minutes. Turn off the heat and let cool. Yield: One quart.

Falernum

2	cinnamon sticks
4 tsp.	fennel seed
5	pieces star anise
4½ tsp.	coriander seeds
1 tsp.	cloves, whole
7 oz.	almond slivers
1 qt.	sorbet syrup

Pan-roast all dry ingredients and fold into sorbet syrup, then refrigerate. Macerate for a minimum of four days, then strain.

Mixed Drink

1 oz.	fresh lime juice
2 oz.	homemade falernum
½ oz.	Cointreau
1 oz.	spiced rum
1 oz.	dark rum
2	pieces fresh ginger root $\frac{1}{16}$-inch thick and 1-inch diameter)
1	lime wedge

Put first six ingredients into a martini shaker. Squeeze lime and leave wedge in with cubed ice. Shake and strain drink into an 11-ounce martini glass. Float a piece of thinly sliced fresh ginger root on top. Garnish with two frozen fresh pineapple cubes and a sprig of fresh mint.

Upcountry Maui Mai Tai

The Hāli'imaile General Store

⅓ oz. liliko'i syrup
1½ oz. light rum
½ oz. orange curaçao
        and ½ oz. orgeat, combined
2 oz. pineapple juice
2 oz. guava juice
¾ oz. dark rum

Fill a 10-ounce glass with ice. Add the liliko'i syrup to create a nice amber look on the bottom of the glass. Add the light rum and orgeat/orange curaçao combination. Pour the pineapple juice along the side of the glass. Pour the guava juice along the side of the glass. Float dark rum (you should now see four distinct layers). Garnish with a lime wedge.

Kon Tiki Ports Mai Tai

Fairmont Kea Lani

½ oz. honey
½ oz. fresh lime juice
 2 oz. orange juice
½ oz. dark rum
½ oz. Bacardi 151 Rum
½ oz. Jamaican rum
        Dash of cocktail bitters
        Dash of ground ginger root
        Dash of Pernod

Mix all ingredients in a shaker with ice. Pour into a glass. Garnish with a pineapple wedge, a maraschino cherry and a paper parasol.

The Tradewinds

RumFire, Sheraton Waikīkī

1 ½ oz. Matusalem Platino Rum
  1 oz. Marie Brizzard Watermelon
        Splash of Soho Lychee liqueur
  1 oz. sweet-and-sour

Combine all ingredients in a cocktail shaker and shake with ice. Strain and serve in a chilled martini glass. Garnish with a cube of watermelon and lemon zest.

Kimo's Mai Tai

Embassy Suites - Waikīkī Beach Walk

1 oz.	peach schnapps
1½ oz.	peach purée
1 oz.	pineapple rum
½ oz.	Bacardi 151 Rum
	Splash of pineapple juice
1 oz.	orange rum
½ oz.	Mandarin orange purée
	Splash of sweet-and-sour
	Splash of dark rum

Fill 16-ounce glass with ice. Mix peach schnapps and peach purée in a blender and pour into the glass to make the first layer. Blend pineapple rum, 151 rum and pineapple juice, and pour into the glass to make the second layer. Blend orange rum, Mandarin orange purée, and sweet-and-sour, and pour into the glass to make the third layer. Should be served frozen and layered. Float dark rum. Garnish with a peach wedge, an orange wheel and a maraschino cherry.

Mai Tai Madness

Planet Hollywood Honolulu

1½ oz. Cruzan Mango Rum
 4 oz. mango purée
       Splash of pineapple juice
       Splash of guava juice
½ oz. DeKuyper Strawberry Passion
       Schnapps

Mix all ingredients, except the schnapps, with ice in a blender. Pour into a 14-ounce glass and top with schnapps. Garnish with a pineapple wedge and a maraschino cherry.

Smooth Shredder

Kōloa Rum

1 oz.   Matusalem Platino Light Rum
1   Hawaiian vanilla bean, crushed
¼ oz.   rock candy syrup or simple syrup
½ oz.   orange curaçao
        Juice of fresh lime
        Juice of fresh Meyer lemon juice
1 oz.   Black Seal Dark Rum

Pour light rum, vanilla bean, syrup and orange curaçao, in order, into a Collins glass. Almost fill with equal parts of lime and Meyer lemon juices. Add dark rum. Do not stir! Garnish with a sprig of mint.

Mango'd Mai Tai Blues

Hukilau Sports Bar & Grill

1 oz.	mango purée
1 oz.	rum
½ oz.	coconut rum
2 oz.	pineapple juice
2 oz.	orange juice
8	fresh blueberries
1 oz.	sour mix
½ oz.	dark rum

Pour the mango purée in a 12-ounce glass. Put rum, coconut rum, juices, five blueberries and sour mix in a shaker tin with ice. Shake vigorously. Gently empty contents into glass and float dark rum on top. Garnish with an orchid and remaining three blueberries.

Toni's Hawaiian Mai Tai

Daniel Thiebaut's Restaurant

	Li hing mui powder
1 oz.	light rum
1 oz.	orange juice
1 oz.	pineapple juice
1 Tbsp.	grenadine
1 Tbsp.	liliko'i or mango purée
¼ oz.	dark rum

Dip rim of a glass in li hing mui powder. Put ice in glass and add first three ingredients, in the order listed, to make layers. Add grenadine and purée. Do not stir! Float dark rum. Garnish with a lime wedge.

Mai Tai Cheesecake

recipegoldmine.com

Toasted Coconut Crust

1 ¾ c. flaked coconut
3 Tbsp. butter, melted

In a small bowl stir together coconut and butter until well combined. Press the mixture evenly onto the bottom of a greased nine-inch springform pan. Bake at 350°F for twelve to fifteen minutes or until golden. Set aside.

Mai Tai Filling

24 oz. cream cheese
¾ c. granulated sugar
5 tsp. cornstarch
4 eggs
1 egg yolk
⅓ c. frozen orange juice concentrate, thawed
¼ c. grenadine syrup
¼ c. orange-flavored liqueur
¼ c. light rum
2 tsp. vanilla extract

continued on next page

In a large bowl combine cream cheese, sugar and corn- starch. Beat with an electric mixer until smooth. Add eggs and egg yolk, one at a time, beating well after each addition. Beat in orange juice concentrate, grenadine syrup, liqueur, rum and vanilla extract. Pour the filling over the crust. Bake at 350°F for 15 minutes. Lower the temperature to 200°F and bake for 1 hour and 10 minutes or until the center no longer looks wet or shiny. Remove the cake from the oven and run a knife around the inside edge of the pan. Chill, uncovered, overnight.

Orange Glaze

½ c.	frozen orange juice concentrate, thawed
4 tsp.	lime juice
4 tsp.	grenadine syrup
1 Tbsp.	cornstarch
1 Tbsp.	orange-flavored liqueur
1 Tbsp.	light rum
	Fresh fruit, sliced

In a small saucepan stir together orange juice concentrate, lime juice, grenadine syrup and cornstarch. Cook and mix until thickened and bubbly. Cook and stir two minutes more. Remove from heat, and stir in liqueur and rum. Drizzle over cheesecake.

Garnish cheesecake with fruit. Chill until serving time. Yield: 12 to 18 slices.

Bibliography and Index

Bibliography

Bergeron, Victor. "Let's Get the Record Straight on the Mai Tai!" *Trader Vic's*, www.tradervics.com/mai-tai-1.html.

Bitner, Arnold and Phoebe Beach. *Hawai'i Tropical Rum Drinks & Cuisine by Don the Beachcomber.* Honolulu: Mutual Publishing, 2001.

Briggs, Joe Bob. "The Great Mai Tai Hunt," *The Joe Bob Report*, www.joebobbriggs.com/maxgolf/mg200010.html.

Broom, Dave. *Rum.* New York: Abbeville Press Publishers, 2003.

Chapman, Tom. "The Sweet and Sour Saga of the Mai Tai," *Spirit of Aloha*, September/October 2006, pages 54-62.

Coulombe, Charles. *Rum: The Epic Story of the Drink That Conquered the World.* New York: Citadel Press, 2004.

Curtis, Wayne. *And a Bottle of Rum: A History of the New World in Ten Cocktails.* New York: Crown Publishers, 2006.

Hess, Robert. "Mai Tai," *Drink Boy*, www.drinkboy.com/cocktails/recipes/MaiTai.html.

Hess, Robert. "Mixology Research: The Mai Tai," *Drink Boy*, www.drinkboy.com/Essays/MaiTai.html.

"Rum Education," *The Rum Club*, www.therumclub.com/rum_education.phtml

"Search for the Perfect Mai Tai," *The Water Blog*, www.papaya.net/wordpress/?p=52

Williams, Ian. *Rum: A Social and Sociable History.* New York: Nation Books, 2005.

Index

Photo Credits

About the Author

Cheryl Chee Tsutsumi is an award-winning travel journalist who has covered Hawai'i for numerous Mainland and local publications, including *Copley News Service, Fodor's, Travel + Leisure, Contra-Costa Times, Chicago Sun Times, Fort Worth Star-Telegram, Honolulu Star-Bulletin, Hawai'i, Hawai'i Westways, Hawaiian Style* and *Modern Luxury*. She is the author of 11 books about Hawai'i; *The New-Wave Mai Tai* is her second title for Watermark Publishing. A lifelong Honolulu resident, Tsutsumi has visited Australia, Bali, Canada, England, Guam, Hong Kong, Italy, Japan, The People's Republic of China, Macau, Majuro, Ponape, Saipan, American and Western Samoa, Tahiti, Taiwan, Tonga, Wales, and many destinations throughout Hawai'i and the continental United States. When she's not researching and writing stories, you'll usually find her at Hilltop Equestrian Center in Waimānalo where she is an avid student of dressage.